old friends

great dogs on the good life

TEXT AND PHOTOGRAPHY BY MARK J. ASHER

CHRONICLE BOOKS

SAN FRANCISCO

To Humphrey, for leading me here.

Text copyright © 2003 by Mark J. Asher
Photographs copyright © 2003 by Mark J. Asher
All rights reserved. No part of this book
may be reproduced in any form without written
permission from the publisher.

Library of Congress Cataloging-in-Publication Data:
Asher, Mark J. Old friends : great dogs on the good
life/text and photos by Mark J. Asher.
p. cm.
ISBN 0-8118-4002-6 (hardcover)
1. Dogs–Pictorial works. 2. Photography of dogs. I. Title.
SF430 .A77 2003
636.7'022'2–dc21   2002151432

Manufactured in Singapore.

Designed by Protopod Design
Typeset in Berthold Garamond

Distributed in Canada by Raincoast Books
9050 Shaughnessy Street
Vancouver, British Columbia V6P 6E5

10 9 8 7 6 5 4 3

Chronicle Books LLC
85 Second Street
San Francisco, California 94105

www.chroniclebooks.com

Dogs provide affection without ambivalence, the simplicity of a life free from the almost unbearable conflicts of civilization, the beauty of an existence complete in itself.

—SIGMUND FREUD

After months of squatting, lying, leaning, cajoling, and begging in the pursuit of capturing over forty-five senior dogs on film, my mission is complete. As Humphrey, my eight-year-old German shepherd/chow licks my sore knees back to health, I try to answer the question asked by many over the course of this project—why do a book on old dogs? I suppose seeing my own dog on the verge of being considered a "senior dog" and beginning to slow down provided a good bit of subliminal impetus. But at the same time I began to notice that in our youth-obsessed society older dogs had been left out of television commercials, magazine advertisements, movies, and books, which are dominated by perfectly cute puppies and sprightly young dogs. Just like the older people I've known, older dogs are filled with wisdom, endurance, and patience. I began to wonder what's behind their boundless vitality and spirit. What do they live for? What are *their* longevity secrets? Why not, I thought, use my artistic professional skills to find the answers to these questions and to ensure that, in fact, every dog does have its day!

While photographing dogs certainly has its challenges (be sure to pack a load of patience and a good pair of knee pads), the photo shoots for this book were filled with the adventure, innocence, and joy that dogs bring to our lives. There was Bubba, the resolute English bulldog who was inseparable from the family duck; Ocadash, the irresistible Afghan/Gordon setter who had been adopted just before he would have been put to sleep; and Abby, the angelic Lab who doted over her litter of puppies at the San Francisco SPCA while waiting to be adopted (she was eventually adopted and now enjoys a wonderful home by the beach). I was inspired to learn that many of the dogs I photographed were adopted late in their lives by owners dedicated to giving them a life of comfort, dignity, and lots of love.

In the end I learned many things about older dogs. Although they may be a little slower and a little grayer, older dogs really are no different from younger dogs—they are still driven by new scents, tasty treats, and a need to love and be loved. What they lack in youthful "cuteness," they make up for with soul and a distinguished appearance. What they lack in untamed exuberance, they make up for with stoicism and a gentle spirit.

Dogs don't live quite as long as we do, which makes every moment of their lives even more precious and worth celebrating. I hope these photographs help to shine a little light on their golden years.

—MARK J. ASHER

P.S. Never leave your camera bag on the ground at a dog park. A Jack Russell with the force of a fire hose is liable to let loose.

NEWTON

fifteen years old

Longevity Secrets

~ soft beds
~ hugs from Mom

M O
seventeen years old

Longevity Secret

~ long walks after dinner

OLLIE
ten years old

Longevity Secret

~ **long, slow walks with time to sniff**

ANNA

eleven years old

Longevity Secrets

~ being a mixed breed: it gives me the best of all worlds
~ getting pets from everyone who passes by

MOLLIE

eleven years old

Longevity Secrets

~ tennis balls—gnawed, pawed, and wet
~ treats—morning, noon, and night

CLINTON
ten years old

Longevity Secrets

~ keeping up with Ginger, the pit bull pup
~ nibbling on Gretel, the cat

LEGGS

eleven years old

Longevity Secret

~ wearing my Burberry coat

JESTER
twelve years old

Longevity Secrets

~ snuggling with my "cuddle buddy," Buttercup the bunny
~ doing yoga, especially my "downward-facing dog" pose

MORGEY
fourteen years old

Longevity Secret

~ **one baby aspirin a day**

NIGEL
nine years old

Longevity Secrets

~ hearing the sound of a tennis ball canister being opened
~ two walks a day, rain or shine

TYGGY
ten years old

Longevity Secrets

~ sit rather than stand
~ sleep rather than sit
~ if you can't sit or sleep, eat

JINKS

eleven years old

Longevity Secrets

~ find a mortal enemy and do battle every day
~ if you're going to break the rules, do it when no one is looking
~ whine until you get what you want

BAILEY
twelve years old

Longevity Secrets

~ be mischievous—only the good die young
~ make time to stop, smell, and eat the flowers
~ sleep soundly, snore loudly

BETTEY
twelve years old

Longevity Secrets

~ providing "love therapy" at my local nursing home
~ feline companionship

ABBY
eleven years old

Longevity Secrets

~ taking time to smell the bushes
~ mentoring young puppies
~ bedtime belly rubs

PETIE
fourteen years old

Longevity Secrets

~ spending time with Maggie, my canine companion
~ hanging at the beach

ZOEY

seven years old

Longevity Secrets

~ demand the royal treatment
~ run wild and reckless in open spaces
~ never save a bone for later

CHICA
twelve years old

Longevity Secrets

~ helping houseguests finish their hors d'oeuvres
~ eating barbecued salmon fresh off the grill

MAX
twelve years old

Longevity Secrets

~ beach parties
~ long days at the dog park

THEO

ten years old

Longevity Secrets

~ **home-cooked meals**
~ **room to roam**

DUELLEY
ten years old

Longevity Secrets

~ **vanilla ice cream**
~ **long truck rides**

PATRICK

ten years old

Longevity Secret

~ when they're handing out bones, come to any name called

OCADASH

sixteen years old

Longevity Secret

~ pancakes drenched in butter

APOLLO
eight years old

Longevity Secrets

~ adding to my sniff-and-squirt tree collection
~ heading up front porch security duty
~ teaching the new puppy how to grow up to be "top dog"

LUCKY AND SHILOH

eleven and ten years old

Longevity Secret

~ **having a best friend**

SAM

twelve years old

Longevity Secrets

~ **Lucy, the golden retriever next door**
~ **long summer days at the lake**

KELSEY

eleven years old

Longevity Secrets

~ roll in smelly things
~ never let little dogs with bows in their hair get the best of you

TONTO
twelve years old

Longevity Secrets

~ sniff where no dog has sniffed before
~ lie in the grass, dig in the dirt, roll in manure, and swim in every pond you can find
~ lift and pee, lift and pee, lift and pee on every tree

BUBBA
twelve years old

Longevity Secret

~ **palling around with the family duck**

COCO
ten years old

Longevity Secret

~ **always accessorize**

LIO
eleven years old

Longevity Secret

~ checking out the finely perfumed ladies

JAGADY

eleven years old

Longevity Secrets

~ cashews in bed
~ playing Monkey in the Middle

VINNIE
fifteen years old

Longevity Secrets

~ start your day early—you'll log more laps around the yard
~ make friends with every dog you meet

SCOOTER
thirteen years old

Longevity Secrets

~ three strong legs and a can-do attitude
~ regular baptisms in ice-cold mountain lakes

FRED
sixteen years old

Longevity Secret

~ **taking time to smell each blade of grass**

HENLEY

eleven years old

Longevity Secrets

~ the eternal search for virgin smells
~ long rolls on my back in the grass

JACKIE
twelve years old

Longevity Secrets

~ assume all food is yours until proven otherwise
~ nap often, snore loudly, and twitch with wild abandon
~ master the art of tug-of-war

TEGAN
fourteen years old

Longevity Secrets

~ look cute and be stubborn—it will get you everything
~ always be first at the door: front door, car door, refrigerator door

WALLY
thirteen years old

Longevity Secrets

~ acupuncture
~ organic chicken

FRED
sixteen years old

Longevity Secrets

~ drinking beer
~ chasing cats
~ running from raccoons

NACHO
ten years old

Longevity Secrets

~ outwitting the pack by running under the big dogs
~ cocking my ears for post-mischief treats

MOLLY

thirteen years old

Longevity Secrets

~ family
~ nine solid hours of beauty rest
~ trips to the beach—the more, the merrier

JASPER

thirteen years old

Longevity Secrets

~ being the first to sample all the food
~ listening to Duke and Ella in the afternoons

POODIE

ten years old

Longevity Secrets

~ digging a hole a day—it keeps the vet away
~ freshly baked pound cake
~ good conversation

HUEY
eighteen years old

Longevity Secrets

~ remember that size is no obstacle to desire
~ lick the hand that feeds you
~ every day is worth wagging your tail about

ACKNOWLEDGMENTS

To my sweet Humphrey, who withstood the jealousy of smelling other dogs on me day after day when I came home from photo shoots. Thanks for keeping your tail wagging during the good times and your paws crossed during the tense times.

To all my four-legged friends who gave their time and attention when they'd rather have been sniffing, licking, fetching, digging, or devouring a big ol' juicy bone: I hope I've done you justice in capturing your beautiful spirit, grace, and wisdom. Be sure to thank your owners for the ride to the shoot and for their gracious help and patience.

To Chronicle Books for giving me the opportunity to do work that gave me the deepest gratification I've ever known. Special thanks to Jack for believing, to Shoshanna for seeing me through, and to Azi for making it all look good.

My deepest appreciation to the following folks, whose selflessness and enthusiasm were a big part in making this project possible: Fabian Gonzalez, Melissa Miller, Jackie King, Jeannie Strongin, Dave Handler, Rachel Markowitz, and Topper the Cat; Doggie Styles and Alpha Dog in Mill Valley; the San Francisco SPCA, BADRAP (Bay Area Doglovers Responsible About Pitbulls), and Pet Camp in San Francisco; and Second Chance Rescue in Marin County, California.